49 THINGS ABOUT ENTREPRENEURSHIP

THAT EXPERTS DO NOT WANT YOU TO KNOW

SAHAR ANDRADE, MB. BCH

Contents

INTRODUCTION

Every small business starts with a dream. But, it takes more than ideas to achieve your goals. Businesses need the knowledge and resources to help their dream come to fruition.

If you are reading this, it means you have decided either to start your business or expand it. To both, I say Congratulations on taking that bold step you know is not easy.

Just know that nothing that anyone tells you beforehand prepares you for the roller coaster ride you are about to take, or no one has ever told you about the nightmares that precede the dream.

Startups are not for the faint hearts – 80% of the start-ups fail in the first three years.

The stories about brands exploding on Social Media or otherwise are inspiring but few and far between. The "overnight" success stories usually have long periods of hard work and preparation.

People get to be entrepreneurs for many reasons, and they are ALL valid. Each entrepreneur has their own story.

Most important for entrepreneurs is not to fall into the abyss of getting caught up in the false glamour of entrepreneurship trying to duplicate what made others successful.

Use the successes as inspiration rather than trying to be like someone else or trying to become the next internet sensation.

Just know that no matter what your business or experience is, someone needs your services, or your product and you have more knowledge than someone else that needs your help.

This book is for you if:

- You have ever wanted to quit your 9 to 5 job to start your own business but felt overwhelmed.

- Felt that fear get hold of you, paralyzing you, keeping you in the same place year after year.

- Felt stuck in your comfort zone wanting to move forward but do not know what to do.

- Feel like you have so much potential inside of you, though you do not have clarity on what to do.

- Have ideas to start a business but do not know where to start or what is the first step.

- Need a simple what to do what not to do list assembled through first-hand experience.

If you answered "YES" to any of these questions, then this book is for you on how to start your Entrepreneurial life. *The good news is that Entrepreneurship is a learned ability, so you can actually learn it.*

My Story:

I started my business seven years ago from scratch. I quit my corporate executive job, gave them two weeks' notice, as I could see the writing on the wall. The company I worked for tried to survive the recession but eventually couldn't weather the wave.

My husband encouraged me to start my own business as he felt I was wasting my time working for someone else making them millions of dollars

I had no idea where to begin, I postponed thinking about it during the last two weeks finalizing the responsibilities of my job.

I had heard people talking about business licenses, zoning, business plans, assets, etc. Honestly, I didn't even know where to start.

So, the first day of being an entrepreneur, my alarm went on at the same time of every previous day, but that day I snoozed it a few times, then I shut it off.

I opened my eyes, then told myself "well I have really nothing to do so I can sleep in today". When I woke up I found myself getting busy doing the beds, washing the dishes, vacuuming the floors, cleaning, and cooking. Then it was time for my husband to come home, we had dinner, watched TV, then went to bed.

The day was repeated throughout the whole week, without doing one thing towards my business.

The second week, I thought about choosing a name of the company, my brain went blank, I couldn't think of any names.

Then I thought about what the business would be. Again, my brain went blank. I discussed it with my husband, he asked me to be kind to myself, that it will come to me, that my brain might be trying to take a break.

I looked at networking groups in my area, I went to a few, some were worthless, some were just fine, and some were good. My favorite was "Toastmasters," it helped a lot with my public speaking and presentation skills

I decided that every day I will wake up early, change into a professional attire, sit on my desk till noon then have my lunch hour and continue working till 5 PM.

I did this every single day, either I had something to do or not. I would research trying to find what is the next step to start my new business. I started branding myself as a product, I used all the experience I had accumulated throughout the years of international marketing.

I started a new Biography, drafted a statement of capability, took a professional picture, I enrolled in one of the first classes of Social Media and got certified as a "Social media" strategist.

Social Media was brand new, many fought it or didn't know about it, I used it every single day. I used LinkedIn every day, I spent two hours a day answering 50 questions in what used to be the "Q&A forum" to build a name.

I answered the questions as if I was helping a paid client, I built a name on the platform.

I connected with conference organizers, journalists, and executives and spent the whole first year building relationships, and bartering services.

I did many nationally syndicated radio interviews, appeared in articles in national magazines, and booked few gigs for Public Speaking.

I did it all for free, but by the end of the first year and beginning of the second, I had built a real strong portfolio that showed credibility. I also recorded a few videos and put them on YouTube and shared them like crazy.

I accidentally found out that I can apply for SBE Certification or Certified Small Business by the State of CA, then turned around and got certified by the LA County based on that. Meanwhile, I also realized that I needed NAISC codes to subscribe to the different bids based on my business.

By the beginning of the third year, I won my first real big government contract, everything after that is history.

The first year and a half I worked between 16 and 18 hours a day/ seven days a week, to where it almost cost me my family. I realized what I needed to do through a lot of trials and errors, with sweat and tears but I made it.

During this journey, I went through so many roller coasters and up and downs, some days I was ready to conquer the world and some days I just wanted to hide, stay in bed and watch the Housewives.

There are a lot of things I wish someone would have told me prior to diving head first into entrepreneurship. Every time I went through a new experience, I promised myself that I will share it with others, then I would forget until the next experience.

So, I decided to write this book, that is not a Shakespearian piece of art or a piece of literature, a simple book from the heart to share the nightmare I went through before I achieved my dream of success, hopefully, it will help in your entrepreneurial journey.

My goal is for those considering becoming entrepreneurs to understand what they are getting into. Success is never an accident or good luck or fortune. As entrepreneurs, we take that big decision to sacrifice a few things to build a business and work hard no matter what it takes.

I wanted to share the painful realistic parts and the high points of success and glamour in 49 things that gurus and experts do not talk about, as there will be days where you will feel like giving up, or you will feel like you are failing, and some days you will feel like you are in top of the world.

Ready for the journey? Buckle up!

1

Entrepreneurship is not easy, success doesn't happen overnight; often things didn't work out the way I expected or planned for it.

Heck, the first business card I ever had didn't even have my company's present name, the second business card showed a job title I don't do anymore – I was still finding my way.

Throughout the years, especially the first two years, I bought book after book, I listened to dozens of gurus, bought numerous programs from experts for thousands and thousands of dollars, money I didn't have; but each new program came with the hope that I will achieve wealth and make six figures after 5 or 8 weeks or whatever they were promising.

Most experts and gurus, sell the dream, the success, or the destination without taking you step by step through the journey. The actual steps of the journey get in the way.

It is easy to dream but, executing that dream is a nightmare most of the time till you get to live the dream.

The experts just describe the end result with all the glory, so hopefuls start these programs all hyped up just to fall flat as they were not warned or prepared for the challenges, obstacles, and difficulties they would meet.

I was one of those hopefuls. Until I learned the hard way it is never a 1-2-3 step and voilà you are there.

I realized that most entrepreneurs follow experts and hang to their every word and opinion, but the Gurus, Experts, and the media are making entrepreneurship sound very exciting to undertake; as if they were taking a trip around the world on a magic carpet. They have been selling the dream without even bringing to attention the obstacles, challenges, and heartaches you must go through to reach success.

They prey on your fears, and dreams and spin their products and programs to appeal to you as if it was your only way out and you believe it, you are not alone. I went personally through it, I was sucked through that endless labyrinth buying more programs and up-sells hoping that the next upgrade or the next step or piece of information will work and will bring me the riches they have been promising.

Now, I learned to read the very tiny fine prints on any program, before I even look at the broad strokes of any program

Hope and fear sell. But sharing setbacks, challenges, efforts, and heartaches will not, that is why they are hidden.

"There are many reasons why 80% of the businesses fail in the first three years."

The main reason is that Entrepreneurs are not prepared for the tough journey ahead, Gurus and Experts want to sell you the good, without the bad and the ugly.

As a result, Entrepreneurs start with unrealistic expectations of what is needed to succeed, as far as money, time and effort are concerned, or how long it takes to get a business off the ground. There is no way to predict when or even if the business will succeed.

Some entrepreneurs can be easily discouraged and give up too soon after encountering an obstacle or two.

Entrepreneurship is not for the faint or weak heart – this is not meant to scare you away from becoming an entrepreneur; it is about giving you the keys to unlock the secrets that no one wants to share that lead to your success and achieving the dream.

Yes, 80% fail but 20% succeed the only common factor in either succeeding or failing is **YOU**, how well prepared you are, how hard you are willing to work, and how far you will go to face the obstacles. It is doable, it is not an impossible mission it is possible

We own our own future, we are the creator of our success, only "US" can decide the next step, to go through the nightmare that leads to the DREAM, only "US" can design our future to transform our self from a caterpillar to a butterfly.

I looked for and found the light at the end of the tunnel, I made a list of things that no one else will share with you nor want you to know so you keep on buying programs and chase the shadows of the dream

I believe that if we know what to expect from the beginning we can be prepared for the good, bad and ugly, it could change everything and lead us to the path of success.

I have helped hundreds of entrepreneurs and startups and received "*Congressional recognition*", I wanted to help more people, as may be an idea I share can strike a new concept for them or help them take the proper steps or make a better decision.

2

WHAT IS ENTREPRENEURSHIP?

As in everything in life that looks like a mystery, there are myths around entrepreneurship. And as with any other endeavor, there are challenges and opportunities. In my "49 things about entrepreneurship that Gurus and Experts do not want you to know; I will be sharing, though not all, the most important challenges as well as some of the major mistakes to avoid.

My intention is that by the end of this book; "**YOU**" the reader will have increased clarity in discovering yourself, exercise better relationships with others, and increase your chance of business success.

Entrepreneurs have a unique set of mindsets and skills that combined create success. It is a learned ability, so we can all learn to become successful entrepreneurs but we must be attentive to the environments around us

The best skill an entrepreneur can learn and apply is the "**Speed of implementation**" which means applying whatever you learn right away and use it immediately especially if you have a great idea do not let it die or wait around implement what you learn.

Entrepreneurs also must develop a new set of **leadership skills** to create more value for their clients and their business, they must become more efficient, and productive through personal leadership.

They must **create valuable products or services** and market them to the proper audience or segment market, the way they chose to be marketed to, using cross-cultural marketing

They are continuously learning how to develop the business and execute the business needs for innovation every day

Entrepreneurs **take action,** they do not just think and plan, but actually get out and do the work, they do not skip a beat to implement their learning, they take what they learn in new ways and put them into action, they begin to feel, think and act differently.

DEFINITION OF ENTREPRENEURSHIP

An entrepreneur always looks for 3 or 4 alternatives to any idea, product or service; they can't be closed minded just for one idea (their own) to succeed.

1- **Entrepreneur**: Comes from a French word meaning undertaking or self-motivation (Entre) connect things build or self-motivate to create a business.

2- They are managers, owners or innovative people that **run a business**. Someone that starts a business. Creates or offer values for customers.

3- Most important, they are **risk takers** they leave the safety of the "status quo" and comfort of the world they know to take a risk towards success. Human beings are programmed to avoid change or avoid loss; it is normal for human beings to be prudent to protect themselves – but entrepreneurs overcome the tendency to play safe and they take calculated risks repeatedly till they create opportunities.

4- **They commit:** Things do not always work as expected, so when things get tough; entrepreneurs must keep going they commit their time, life and money take risks to succeed. Most people get too attached and emotionally involved with their own ideas and sometimes get tunnel vision.

5- **Make or create value for other people**: Entrepreneurs learn what is desired, wanted, needed by other people mainly their customers or what are the fears and frustrations the customers want to avoid so they offer value through their products or services to become a successful business.

6- **They are creators**: They do not just adapt to the environment, they create their own environment it takes wisdom to create new things – they create jobs for others – they create their own world and worlds for others.

7- **They have their identity and self-image** and who they are becoming in a new world, they label themselves as entrepreneurs, they envision themselves as an actual person operating in a world waiting to be shaped or helped by someone like themselves – they take initiatives and they get rewards.

Successful entrepreneurs are defined as people who, with vision and hard work, have achieved a measure of control over their own destinies.

Success is meant to be covering all areas of their life as an entrepreneur both personal and professional

Every entrepreneur has their own styles of entrepreneurship. It is affected by their background experiences, cultures, and vision, mission and core values.

Many factors can determine their entrepreneurial style. Their entrepreneurial style is created by a complex set of behaviors and attitudes that impact their flexibility or rigidity when facing obstacles and achieving tasks, and how they solve problems and offer customer service.

Entrepreneurs create profitable businesses. They must know "**WHY**" they are an entrepreneur.

3

WHY DO PEOPLE WANT TO BE ENTREPRENEURS?

The biggest reward of becoming an entrepreneur is to have the satisfaction that comes from making their own decisions and acting on them. People become entrepreneurs for many reasons:

- They want to have the freedom to make their own rules

- They must achieve dreams they know they can't achieve while being an employee

- They hate what they currently do

- They want to reach their full potential

- They want to make more money as there is no limit to what the entrepreneur can make

- They do not want to have a boss anymore

- They must build a better future

- They feel stagnated where they are

- They want to make the world a better palace

MYTHS AROUND ENTREPRENEURSHIP

- Being in full control

- Be my own boss

- Work on my own schedule

- Have less stress

- Calling themselves "President or CEO" make people think they are a big corporation

- Making tons of money from day one or become a millionaire within a year

- Work on a beach, while money is added to their bank account from the get-go.

Risks of Entrepreneurship

- Alienation from social life, family, and friends

- Cash flow and finances: Any start-up business takes a while to start making money either for expansion, profits or salaries

- Potential Failure: Nothing is guaranteed and there are no safety nets

- Challenges and problems

Challenges:

80% of the businesses fail in the first three years-

1- Money or the lack of it

2- Doing everything themselves. Not trusting anyone

3- Building a sustainable infrastructure system

4- Long working hours causing isolation

5- Working alone can cause stress and depression

6- Getting wrapped in their own heads and ideas failing to analyze the market

7- Procrastination or Wanting perfection

8- Having ideas not executing them

9- Can be too forceful or too impatient

10- Can be insensitive to others, or forceful

11- Can bog down in details and lose time

12- Can be critical and finicky, or sensitive to feedback

13- Can seem to lack courage

ARE YOU READY?

1. Are you ready to have no paycheck for a while?

2. Are you ready to dig into your own savings to start?

3. Are you ready to wear many hats simultaneously?

4. Are you ready to hustle every day?

5. Are you ready to work long hours; sometimes not seeing results immediately?

6. Are you ready to become a leader?

7. Do you have expertise and credibility?

8. Are you resilient?

9. Are you self-disciplined?

10. Are you ready for sacrifices initially?

11. Are you ready to find or have mentors?

12. Are you ready to find a good support system?

13. Are you ready to become a good communicator?

4

CHARACTERS OF AN ENTREPRENEUR

Being an entrepreneur requires certain traits and characteristics unique to them, these are some of their must-have characteristics to succeed:

1- **Have the courage to explore their curiosity:** Curiosity leads to innovation and creativity. Courage doesn't mean lack of fear it is rather acting despite the fear.

2- **Risk Takers**: Risks are the chances to lose something so risks must be calculated. They take the initiative to gain an advantage. Entrepreneurs learn to take decisions even when they are uncertain. Paying their bills and taking care of their families will depend on these decisions, as they do not have the comfort of a paycheck anymore. The decisions will directly affect them like hiring, expanding or not, outsourcing, etc.

3- **Have to be hungry all the time**: Entrepreneurs must be hungry to succeed, and it doesn't stop, if they are not hungry they will not hustle, and they can't stop hustling no matter what.

Being an entrepreneur takes hustle; hustling is not about forcing yourself to keep pushing or about adding more stress to your life.

Being constantly hungry doesn't mean being greedy or money hungry. A very important principle states: "*If you do not ask, you do not get and if you don't ask you lose 100% what you might get; if you ask your chances to get what you asked for is 50/50*".

4- **Know where to start**: They must start by getting good support around them: Working by themselves can make them feel lonely and cut off and can take them down depression road especially initially where they can feel alienated. The antidote is waking up every day feeling they are living their passion, and knowing their "why"

5- **Self-Control while being adaptable and flexible**: They must be structured and self-disciplined: Especially if they work from home. They must decide on their hours of operations, wake up on time, dress professionally, not stopping during working hours to take care of any chores in the house or pay a bill unless after work hours or during lunch hour as if they were working for someone else. Yes, they have their freedom to do what they want to do; when they want to do; it but freedom always come at a cost. They know how to adapt to different scenarios and are flexible to change and adjust their goals whenever needed.

6- **Have mental strength**: They will be challenged and stressed. They must learn how to release that stress, how it manifests in them and what and when it happens. Controlling their emotions will work best for them. Starting with breathing technics, some mindfulness exercises, and meditation can work best for them. They must start their days the right way, get into a morning routine that will energize their day's productivity. They say the first 30 minutes define the rest of the day.

7- **Have Perseverance & Determination**: Not letting obstacles stop them. Life will throw its curve balls every now and then. Only they can choose how to react to them, if they persevere in their own path, their mindset towards success will become stronger by the day. They learn from challenges considering them as a stepping stone from which they bounce back.

8- **Tough and thick-skinned**: They know they might fail sometimes, barriers and surprises will get in the way – They know they can overcome all that. They know that they will never be the cup of tea for everyone and it is fine by them, they accept the fact they can't be everything to everyone.

9- **Self-Awareness**: They know who they are and what they represent, they know their products, their market, and their audience's niche and they accept and realize that they are not Jack of all trades (Master of none). They are self-confident and know when they must ask for help.

10- **Hard workers**: They know their destiny is between their own two hands if anything happens there is no one else to blame but themselves. Eventually, they will find their work-life balance to avoid their families' suffering from the long hours they put into their new business. It is advisable that before embarking on their journey entrepreneurs must enlist their tribe's help and support and prepare them for what is coming.

5

10 MINDSET SHIFTS YOU HAVE TO HAVE TO BECOME A SUCCESSFUL ENTREPRENEUR

Many think that an entrepreneur's life is glamorous and success happens overnight, but it's actually a lot of hard work.

1. Money What?

Get comfortable with money: Talking about it, sharing your rates or sometimes not having it at all. Sometimes you must spend money to make money,

Invoicing, payments follow-up, and late payments justify your worth.

Many cultures have a *shame feeling* related to "talking about money", women get anxiety speaking about money. They do not know how to ask for it, or how to negotiate their worth.

You must change your relationship with money, you are getting paid not only for your services but for all the education, effort, time and sacrifices you went through life to get to this point. You earned the money and you deserve it, so accept it gratefully.

2. Toot your own horn.

As an entrepreneur, some shameless self-promotion is just a part of the gig. You must learn storytelling to share your story. Your uniqueness will lie in your own story. If you do not toot your own horn no one else will. It is not about being self-centered and is not about blatant self-advertising. You must share what you do, to who and your values. Your message must be clear and concise, so your target market will understand your message and what you do and how it affects them and their lives. Only then you can build fruitful Business relationships.

3. Light your own fire.

As an entrepreneur, you must be a self-starter and a self-motivator. No more security blankets. Your success will originate from your own motivation to move forward. It starts and ends with you. You are the only one that can propel you forward, you might get help every now and then but you can't depend on that.

You can only depend on you, or you can get into your own way, depending on how much you want to achieve your success.

You will face a lot of ups and downs, your resilience and commitment are what will determine your future.

4. Say goodbye to 9-5.

One of the biggest myths is that entrepreneurship offers you the control over your schedule, you make up your own hours, and you will not do 9 to 5 anymore.

Initially, you must put between 10 and 15 hours a day to help build the foundation of your business, especially in the first 12 to 18 months.

Building a direction and deciding which way to go will take a lot of work and effort. Maintain your productivity by taking short breaks between.

5. **Give the sizzle not the steak.**

You must be able to quantify the value you can provide- This is sales and marketing 101. I remember the first proposal I sent to a prospective client I had enclosed a lot of fine details and processes, and how I would execute the proposal.

The client took my proposal and the step by step plan then applied it themselves and I lost the contract, plus my time and effort. This was my biggest lesson in business, my proposals, later on, were done in broad strokes, highlighting the general guidelines to achieve the results rather than the operational details.

6. **Trust in yourself**

You will get unsolicited advice, from everyone around you. Most of the advice is not what you need. Some people will feel threatened when you start your business, you must believe in what you do especially that you will have ups and downs.

Often you will feel like giving up, that nothing is happening, that you might have taken the wrong decision and doubt any decision you took. Success can be just around the corner or just one step away.

7. **You are your OWN brand**

Do not hide behind your business, you can have your business brand, and have your own brand. Your brand creates influence and credibility for your audience to trust you and deal with you.

If you don't know your brand, your brand value, your brand positioning in the market no one else will know.

Your brand is your promise to your customers, either you are a solution that solves a problem for them or you are filling a gap that exists in their lives. You must know where your brand fits and share it.

8. You will never be "Everything" for "Everyone"

There is no way you can be everything for everyone, it is simply impossible. You can never cover a whole market for all its needs. Market segmentation and niching are how to go.

Many entrepreneurs, small business owners, and startups believe that the more they try to market their products or services, the more customers they will get, and more money they will make.

Their message gets diluted and falls on deaf ears. They waste money, effort, time, and sometimes hope.

9. Appearances matter

Dress for success. If you want to reflect success you must show it in everything you do.

The way you dress, the way you brand yourself, the way you talk, even the postings on social media by uncovering a little of your lifestyle online so people can see your success. People judge how you dress, how you appeal even the car you drive. It is superficial, but this is how the world works.

10. Prepare for loneliness for a while

Entrepreneurship is lonely. Starting a business will require long hours mainly working alone in isolation.

It will get lonely and it will get boring, that is why as an entrepreneur your inner motivation and commitment are keys to your success.

Knowing your "WHY" and believing in your purpose will make this lonely time bearable as means to an end.

6

HERE ARE THE **49** THINGS GURUS AND EXPERTS DO NOT WANT YOU TO KNOW ABOUT ENTREPRENEURSHIP

One of the best things you will ever do is to start your own business. Starting a business is exciting but tremendously scary but ALL worth it.

I met hundreds of entrepreneurs that say they will start their business after getting their business plan ready, or after they get funding, or after they get help; as a result, they never start.

Remember that the best way to learn to swim is jumping into the sea, i.e., starting your business, you can't afford to sit around waiting for things to fall perfectly in place. The time to start your business is now.

Some "wannabe" entrepreneurs will keep making excuses for why they never started their business till the day they die and will never achieve their fulfillment and success.

Gurus and experts try to sell you a dream in the format of a program of a few weeks to achieve six figures as if it was a magic pill.

They sell you the dream without the reality and without ever bringing to your attention the nightmare or collection of nightmares you will need to go through before you get to the other side and live your dream

They are hiding the nitty gritty of becoming an Entrepreneur, a startup or a small business owner- they are selling the hope actually a mirage on a hot day rather than actually pointing you to the real well.

So, I made a list of things that no one else will share with you or want you to know so you keep on buying the up-sell and new programs to chase the shadows of the dream.

I am sharing pitfalls, trials and errors I went through building my own business, so you can avoid them. These are things I discovered going through the entrepreneurial journey. Many no one ever mentioned them before. It is first-hand experience and not something read in a book.

We should expect the best, prepare for the worst: No matter when and where you start your business, your product or service must be tweaked or changed along the road.

Change, though the only constant in life, is never comfortable. You must think about the worst-case scenario that can happen, by imagining it and preparing for it only then you can position yourself to try to protect yourself and your business.

Embrace this and look beyond the present conditions to your long-term goals and vision of success.

Gurus and Experts will NEVER tell you that:

1. If you *start your business without defining your own meaning of success and Happiness,* you won't achieve either; or at least not in a way that will please you. First, you must know what success means to you; to have a blueprint of where you want to go. Own your success and not be owned by it.

   If you are a woman (woman-preneur) you need to work twice as hard. People will assume that your success has either been handed to you by a man or you succeeded because of a man.

2. *Everything starts and ends with you.* You can have the best formulas and strategic plans, but if you don't know yourself inside out, your strengths and your weaknesses, what motivates you, what inspires you and how you can use your personal leadership to grow and lead others, chances are slim that you reach your ultimate goals.

   You must know yourself, inside out, before knowing your business. You are the master of your universe, without self-awareness any plans are worth nothing.

3. *There will be failures before the success:* You will fail at something sooner or later. If you do not fail then you are not taking enough risk.

Just being an entrepreneur doesn't guarantee success. Failure is inescapable and it will come in many different shapes and forms so be ready, and embrace it. You are likely to make a few or a lot of mistakes which will cause setbacks.

How you look at failure or setback will determine if you succeed or not. If you look at failure as the end of the road, then good luck, but if you look at a setback and think that "*now I know what not to do next time and let me learn the lesson I am supposed to learn here*" to move forward.

Sometimes it takes failure to learn what you don't know and start learning the fundamentals you need to build your business right.

Your ability to rise above them will eventually lead you to success.

If you anticipate that mistakes will happen, you will be better prepared for them, will bounce faster, and be more prepared emotionally for setbacks. It is all about risk mitigation, most mistakes or failure will be self-induced from our self-limiting beliefs.

4. *Entrepreneurship is a learned ability and a lifestyle* that might or might not bring riches. You are continuously bombarded with the best and newest programs and blueprints from Gurus and experts that are supposed to make you six figures in a few weeks, depending on who is selling the program. It doesn't happen that way.

Entrepreneurs are a different breed of people, with different ways of thinking, and behaviors, with different wants and needs.

As there is no set path to success, every entrepreneur, startup, and small business owner has different ways of doing things, though basic entrepreneurial guidelines exist,

The business you start will inevitably evolve and differ from the original concept or idea. To succeed and keep the success you must continuously adapt to the changing market needs, if not it is "sayonara". Nothing is set in stone, expect change and embrace it. Your flexibility to change and to adapt will determine your success or will frame your failure.

Go with the flow; Entrepreneurship can make you happy and fulfilled, it can also make you money, not right away, but you will get there if you stick at it.

5. Make *personal development a priority for yourself.* The only real value and biggest asset of your business is "YOU". As your business grows and expands, you can no longer depend on only your current understandings and skill sets. You must grow to match the growth of your business and ideas.

Taking the time to work on your own self-development is the biggest corner of your success. It can represent a challenge for the entrepreneur. It is the only way to embrace the continuous change that comes with entrepreneurship, either in economics, environment or technology.

This can help overcome the ups and downs of a growing business. Whether it is looking for your real purpose, understanding your "why", finding your passion or even going through a self-discovery journey; they will all lead to one destination it is your own growth and path that will eventually lead you to success.

6. *Self-Care is a priority*. Self-care is not just another hype movement about feeling Zen. It is about taking care of your own health and well-being.

   As an entrepreneur, you are your business and your business is you, if you go down, your business goes down with you.

   You come first, it is not being selfish or self-centered or being a narcissist, it simply means that if you are not standing on your own two feet, you can never help or support anyone else that depends on you. If you are not in good shape mentally, physically and psychological you are of no help to no one at all levels. If you do not know how to take care of you, no one else will and you cannot take care of anyone else.

   As entrepreneurs we work nonstop, we hustle all the time, as a result, we forget to take care of ourselves, we sometimes eat too much or not at all, we do not move much so we lose our flexibility or gain weight and it is a downward spiral from there.

   We believe that we will always have time tomorrow to take care of our self, to work out or eat healthier or go on a diet but tomorrow becomes a repeat of today.

   When we are in great shape, we have more clarity of thinking, more endurance, better productivity and more efficiency.

   We erroneously feel we need to spend every living hour building our business and serving our customers, and we feel guilty if we spend a few minutes either taking care of our self or having fun.

7. *You need to focus on your strength, not your weaknesses*: Your success

will come from spending your time using your strengths, rather than wasting your time shoring your weaknesses. That doesn't mean ignoring your weaknesses, just know what they are and look for help to balance them either by outsourcing, delegating or looking for mentors, consultants or free resources.

You also need to believe in your strength. Self-doubt can hold you back and prevent you from achieving your full potential. Leverage your strength by having curiosity and courage to ask questions that many might fear to ask, as the answers will provide you insight that can add a strength you might not have known that you possessed. We do not know what we do not know till we know.

8. *Your small business can make you small minded-* just because you are starting as a small business doesn't mean you will always stay small. All big businesses started somewhere. Your mindset is crucial at this stage.

If you live with a scarcity mind where you feel like you do not have enough of anything, guess what? This is what you will get "not enough".

Scarcity mind is the first enemy you need to watch for. It will keep you paralyzed feeling like a victim. Negative mindsets undermine your beliefs that you are capable of greatness.

Do not go down the trail of "**lack of resources**" either money, support, manpower, capabilities, education, etc. as you will start focusing on what you do not have rather than what you have.

This mindset can make you stick to what may not be good for you because your brain tries to protect you from experiencing any pain from loss or change.

Scarcity also diminishes your ability to make decisions. Like a magnet, it pulls you away from focusing on activities that can fuel your growth.

What you focus on grows. If you divert all of your attention to the one circumstance that negatively triggers you, the rest of the positive areas in our life will suffer.

9. The *way you talk to yourself* is fundamental to your results either success or failure.

Never EVER limit your thinking. Do NOT think small as telling yourself "*I JUST want to cover my rent or cover my expenses or just make a $1000.00*".

What you think or what you prime your brain with, is what you will get positive or negative. Do NOT be scared to dream BIG.

The more you will advance, and the more you will succeed, the more doubts and frustrations you will get. You will see your progress, and you will be anxious about keeping moving forward and not backward.

Self-doubt, fear and confidence crisis will also become part of your everlasting shadow.

Self-doubt is something we all experience. However, success cannot be achieved when you believe in self-limiting thoughts and beliefs that sabotage it. Successful people face their limiting beliefs and doubt and move forward with mindfulness, intention, and action. By changing your negative thought patterns, you empower yourself with the belief and worthiness to move forward and create the life you want.

There is no overnight success, it takes years to build. Entrepreneurship is hard work.

10. *Catastrophizing everything* and seeing everything as doom and gloom are NOT what will drive you to success. If this is your way of thinking, what you think this is what you get.

People rather complain than being grateful for what they have or being grateful for the ability to start their business on their own when millions of humans only dream to do it daily.

As an entrepreneur, you must *not only have but keep your optimism*. You will need it. Sometimes you will feel boxed, and nothing will go right or as planned.

You just must know and believe that if you keep your options open, you will always come on the top, there is a way around things. That everything always happens for a good reason even if you don't see it at the time.

Always look at the glass half full; change the negative to positive. Keep looking for solutions to things that frustrate you and others, then you will be on the right track of succeeding in your business.

There will be extreme highs and deep lows it is like a swing up and down, with no middle stop, one day you will feel you are touching the stars and the next you will feel you just want to hide.

Your optimism and faith in yourself and your business will keep you going.

11. You must have *resilience and perseverance* as well as having the mindset "*that no matter what it takes I will persevere, that there is always a way*". There are days you will want to QUIT and go back to a corporate job. Don't think you have lost your entrepreneurial spirit when you have these days. It's normal. Every entrepreneur has these days.

    No matter how dark the night gets the light of morning always has to break through. You must deeply believe that everything either has a solution so you find it no matter what it takes or has no solution so you move on.

    Gurus and experts do not talk about how to look at challenges as opportunities to grow. Know there is always a way. You need to really love and believe in what you do because there will be a lot of naysayers that you will need to deal with.

    Don't give up, don't take anything personally, and don't take "NO" for an answer; you never know what you will learn along the way.

    When someone says "NO", it doesn't mean it will be forever, it is NO now, conditions and environments might change.

12. *Making Fear your friend* is the best weapon you can learn. Fear is and will always be there. Being fearless doesn't mean living without fear but means acting despite fear.

    There are more than 50 types of fears that can chain us to the ground. Fear can be your best motivator, instead of letting fear dominate your life and paralyze you or make you miss on opportunities that could make your future.

Fear masquerades in so many forms, sometimes you will not even be able to recognize it. Some people have fear of failure, failure of success, failure of embarrassment, failure of loss, failure if ridicule, or even imposter syndrome.

But, you can make fear your friend, using it as a window to your future so you can be prepared for whatever comes your way. *"Whether you think you can or whether you think you can't, you're right." Henry Ford*

13. *Family should always come first.* You must set your non-negotiables and your priorities from the get-go.

The first 18 months of my business I worked seven days a week 15 hours a day. Though my husband is my biggest supporter, he felt lonely as I got so obsessed that I wouldn't even go out to dinner sometimes. He went along for a long time, then he shared that he is feeling a distance growing between us. I resisted initially as I was in that tunnel where I could just see the startup of the business.

That weekend we went away together for a mini vacation. I thought about it and knew that without my husband there would have never been a business that his trust and belief in me as well as his support enabled me to start the business and not worry, I had to reconsider my priorities, and my family came first.

Since then, we never had that problem again, I had never thought about it before though it is very logical to consider it, but I was blinded by the need to succeed. It would have never been a success if the business did and lost my family,

At the end, Family is what counts so do not get totally lost in your business and forget your family they are your support, do not neglect them. Keeping your feelings bottled up inside, will alienate you even more.

If no one ever knows what you're thinking or what you need, you can't expect to be understood or even supported.

14. You must *learn when you need help and how to ask for it*. Most of anything you are going through or will go through, someone else has gone through it and probably figured out a way to overcome it or go around it.

   Feeling proud or feeling ashamed to tell someone "*I do not know, can you help me?*", or feeling dependent and weak not knowing what you are doing, can get in the way.

   Some do not ask for help because of a misguided idea of losing control or burdening other people, some even think that they are not equipped to reciprocate the favor.

   This is the beginning of the decline, knowing when to stop what you are doing, and ask for support or assistance is one of the main triggers to success instead of wasting valuable time, resources and money to do nothing.

   As entrepreneurs, we need to be humble enough and accept the fact of being vulnerable sometimes to accepting help from others either as ideas, thoughts, or even physical help.

It's vital for entrepreneurs to know WHO to ask WHAT and WHEN, after doing your own homework and listening to your instincts.

15. You will need and should get *mentors, advisors, or consultants* crucial to your success. "It takes a village".

You can never do it alone, and you will never know everything you need to know, either to start your business or to grow it.

Look for mentors to help you grow in the business and personally, you can have more than two or three mentors in different areas of your life. You will also need advisors either as trusted successful business people, friends or business advisors from services like SCORE or SBDC that help you for free through government resources.

You will also need as you go to hire consultants that can see what you can't at the time helping you to grow and expand.

16. *Ideas themselves are not valuable on their own* or are not worth much. Everyone has ideas that will always remain ideas until they are executed. Gamble with executing your ideas even if they are not a sure thing.

Your ideas should offer something different to your audience as solving a problem or filling a gap in the market.

Starting a business just because an idea appeals to you alone usually is not a great idea (No pun intended).

You must validate it before moving forward with execution, collect feedback and do not dismiss the negative one.

Just know that every idea has a shelf life and a progression cycle.

Change is a natural process and part of that progressive cycle. The more accepting of change you are, the more you will get out of your own way.

An idea will remain an idea and will die on the island of ideas if not executed.

17. As entrepreneurs managing your *own schedule and timetable, you set your own hours as you please, is a myth.* This is far from the truth. There are no set work hours, you will always work, if not physically, mentally.

You will have time off but after a while building your foundation.

You will hustle every single hour of the day, to network, keeping in touch with prospective clients and customers, find and close deals.

Entrepreneurs must stay hungry all the time, not greedy or self-centered but hungry for success. This is the only way to grow and succeed at least for the first years, part of it will stay with you all the time.

Hungry entrepreneurs are passionate about their business and are eager (or hungry) to get to work each day.

Hungry entrepreneurs have certain characters that lead them to success. They always follow up, nothing stands in their way to achieve what they set up to do no matter what, they do not believe in excuses, know how to ask for the sale and close it, work on minimal hours of sleep, they know where and with whom to network, and take the time to develop relationships without being pushy.

18. *You will not be your own boss.* I have news for you, every *customer* you acquire will be your boss till you finish the contract, the only difference is that you can control who you want to work with. Customers are the soul of every business, so you must continuously ensure their satisfaction. Customers will influence your work pace, schedule, deadlines, and delivery.

    Your *business* itself will become your boss, and controls you, depending on what you do. There are times you will discard your sleeping schedule, or work overtime, or even forget about your social life and sometimes family. It determines what to do, and even imposes it on you.

    If you have *investors*, they will be your boss. They will represent a higher authority.

19. There is a *dark side to Entrepreneurship*. There is a huge sense of Isolation when you become an entrepreneur and you will miss the office camaraderie.

    Most of the time you will work by yourself, especially the first year or two. You can maintain a balance – you can go for a walk, work at a Starbucks or if you can afford it get one of those co-op office spaces

    More than 80% fail within the first 3 years. If you do not know that, you will not be prepared to face it. Yes, a 80% failing rate, but you can be within the 20% success.

Starting my own business, I never ever thought about the 80%, I went in prepared and did my research so I can steer clear from failure.

This is part of the nightmare that precedes the dream. Get out and make it happen

20. *You will be your business, and your business will be you,* make sure that you reflect your brand, you reflect who you want people to see, make sure you are the image you want to project, that you are the promise you make.

Another mistake for building a business is that most entrepreneurs hide behind their business.

Brands are not only for businesses, you must have your business brand but most important you must have your own personal brand.

Your brand is the perception you want people to have of yourself and of your business, it is the promise you offer your audience. Your brand is what will differentiate you from your competition, it is why your audience will engage with you and not the next person that offers the same service or product you do. You must show others what value you add to their lives.

Your brand is what will determine your Unique Selling Proposition, your value proposition, and the way you will market your business.

Your brand creates influence and credibility for your audience to trust you and deal with you.

21. You will *not become a millionaire overnight.* The fast money-making schemes are a delusion. In entrepreneurship especially in the beginning, the *money* is unpredictable.

    There is no steady flow of income, and you lose the regularity of the paychecks.

    Once you establish yourself you will get a better idea what to expect a month, a quarter, a semester or even a year's income

    You can have the *best laid out plans* and the best intentions, and the best skills but at a certain time, things will not go as planned. Take a deep breath and learn the lesson.

    Entrepreneurship is not a set of steps 1-2-3 and you get there, it is a long winding road, filled with hardship, fun, learning opportunities, happiness, and sadness. You can set to follow a certain path, only to end up somewhere different.

    There is no straight path to entrepreneurship. The biggest mistake entrepreneurs make is to attempt to make sense of the business through structured business plan and strategies we all know doesn't work that way.

    How you thought your business is or will be; will keep changing. You will just need to go with the flow. An idea or a transaction or even a comment will let you think or conduct business differently. It is all good, you keep learning as you and you go that way. Change is a good thing

22. You must at least *comprehend or become an expert in all business aspects* either you like it or not. Gurus do not tell you you will become your own bookkeeper, your own marketing agent and Public Relation agent, sales agent, your administrator, your own assistant, your scheduler and then the executor, especially initially.

This is a great thing in your entrepreneurial journey, with each function you practice, you get your mind ready to approach the business from a different viewpoint that you might have never thought about before. Then you will be set to change your business for the better.

When you can afford it, in the second or third year then you can outsource, either independent contractors or hire part-time or full-time employees depending on your situation.

But you must understand and know your brand inside out, so you can make sure that your staff implements the proper strategy to take your business where it needs to be.

You can't depend on someone else following your exact vision, you must monitor it and know what to ask for.

You cannot allow your brand to be diluted or misrepresented based on someone else perception of what your vision is.

23. *Passion alone will not cut it*. Passion is a must have, no negotiation about that.

Gurus and Experts tell you "passion is your path to succeed" but they do not tell you it is not enough. Passion alone doesn't pay the bills – you must turn that passion into concrete business, practice it and execute it.

ONLY THEN you can attain the "Flow state" they talk about when they mention passion.

Passion alone might not translate to a viable business concept, do your due diligence and research.

For example, you start a catering company or a restaurant just because you like to cook. Then you discover that running a cooking business involves more than onions and tomatoes or recipes you love to share, it involves customer service, budgeting, marketing, business planning and a lot more.

The first step for most entrepreneurs is to make sure that their business they are passionate about can generate revenues to sustain themselves, if not they will close down and fail.

So, before going down the entrepreneurial road, entrepreneurs must do their research and study to test the need and viability of their business.

24. *Trying to be perfect.* Those who insist on *perfection* get little done as they try to avoid mistakes. Everything worth having. Starts with taking a risk.

Life is about making mistakes, taking chances, and allowing risk.

The only mistake that can hurt you is avoiding living your life.

If you keep waiting until you feel that everything is perfect, you will either do nothing, or someone else will be doing a better job solving your audience's problems.

Perfection on its own definition means you need to release something to perfect it. Perfection comes from procrastination and procrastination is rooted in fear. Inaction is your worst enemy.

You must just start, test your idea, it can be a solid business concept that will make you money, and you can tweak your business as you go and as needed.

Just know there is no perfection in this world, you can thrive to excellence but perfection is a myth that our brain creates camouflaging fear so it will keep us in our comfort zone, preventing us from what it could perceive as danger.

25. *Don't fake it till you make it, but make it till you become it.* We have been hearing this repeatedly, fake it till you make it, it is not true as you always must be authentic and genuine, and not just fake it till you get what you want. Your clients will discover that you are not authentic and won't like it.

Instead, do what you need to do to change till change becomes part of you.

Habits can become automatic if you keep doing them for 21 to 30 days straight, then it becomes part of the real you.

Entrepreneurship is about self-growth, about knowing what we need to move to the next level.

It is not only about what we possess in talents and skills, it is about understanding what upgrades we must keep doing to level the field for our success, to compete properly and serve our audience the way they want to be served.

26. *Get used to rejection*: You will face a lot of rejections especially initially. Rejections can be a blessing in disguise. It is always about how you look at things through which mirror, negative or positive.

We can't control what life throws at us, we can't control others, but we have 100% control on how we receive and react to rejections. Do we look at it as a stepping stone to go back to the drawing board and look at what can be corrected or adapted, or we despair and give up? It is our choice.

Rejection is a temporary detour, not a dead end. Rejection might help you discover blind spots you have, it sure help me find some of mine, it helped me somehow check my ego, made me more humble, and gave me thicker skin. With every rejection I became better at presenting my business, at better pitching my value and passion.

27. *The failing rate of businesses is 80% or more in the first three years.* That is because entrepreneurs start their business unprepared, they think their ideas are the best thing since sliced cheese.

They think that success is about a business and marketing plan, a business concept or structure.

It is less about talent and skills and intellect than it is about YOUR drive. The real reason behind such a high rate of failure is that 80% of the business success is about the entrepreneur or small business owners themselves, their characters, traits, and psychology, and most do not have the gravitas for it. Only 20% is about businesses processes.

Entrepreneurship is not a job or a title it is more about mindset and a mind shift than about processes, you can be the smartest person in the world, the most talented in the word or the most skilled at what you do, if you do not have that internal motivation and drive to do more, to achieve more, to succeed more. You will get stuck at a certain point.

Only a few people are mentally, psychologically and emotionally ready for the entrepreneurship risks and challenges.

28. Entrepreneurs *get bogged down in details* of their products or their services, they focus on the process and details on how their product work, or how they offer their services. They lose their audience. They must pay more attention to the bigger picture.

The audience never cares about the process you went through to offer your products or services and they care less about the process to make it work. All that they care about is how your product or service will add value to their lives, or how it will help them solve a problem they have. The audience cares about end results and not how to get there.

Too many details will zoom them out, and they will bounce to another product or service that delivers the result with little effort from their part to use it.

Entrepreneurs must stay focused and not get sidetracked by little details.

Know your customer's priorities, this way you will minimize wasting time on things that can eat up your time versus things that will add to your bottom line business progress and revenues.

29. *People will disappoint you or will not show up for you.* Every now and then, you will need praise o – just be prepared that you might not get it.

As you go through your entrepreneurial journey, you will discover who cares about you and your success.

Some people will not understand your hard work and sometimes self-imposed isolation; they will give up on you.

You will try to depend or rely on some people who will let you down or will not show up for you.

You might look for physical help, or someone making introductions for you or lending you some money, or you expect them to be patient with you, or you want them to understand you, or to help you succeed.

Understand that when you look to other people for motivation or support you are looking at a variant outside factor that might or might not come to your rescue or to give you the reassurance you seek internally.

Prepare yourself for all that in advance just in case so it won't hold you back, if and when it happens.

At times, you will need praise to keep going just be prepared again that you might not get it.

If you are lucky enough to have your people always showing up for you and supporting you then you have hit the jackpot

If they don't, you will know next time who to depend on, knowing they are not bad people they are doing what they know best, they are not trying to hurt you, it has to do more of who they are then who you are.

Figuring out whom to avoid and whom to let in won't always be easy.

30. Almost everyone around you *will become a self-proclaimed expert about everything and will give you unsolicited advice.*

Suddenly, everyone around including the people struggling all their life to establish a business or even get a steady job and failed, will advise you on what to do and what not to do, what to expect and what not to expect, though they might be part of the 80% failure rate. You will not even have to ask for opinions they will volunteer.

Some people around you will have purely altruistic reasons to help, either they know or do not know what they are talking about is a different story; and some will have real needs to make money or have delusions about whether they know what they are talking about, or the worst they try to make you fail so you won't be better than them and succeed, misery loves company.

If they are wrong, they rarely hold themselves accountable or even admit they were wrong.

They will justify their wrong opinions or advice as being just off on timing or blindsided by an unlikely event. They have the same inventory of self-justifications that everyone has and are no more inclined than anyone else to revise their beliefs just because they made a mistake.

Always listen with a grain of salt, see if there anything to learn from it and move on as they can waste your time and money.

31. There will *ALWAYS* be haters and Nay-Sayers around you. Those are the people that reflect their unhappiness on you, they don't have the courage to become entrepreneurs and are hating you because you took the risk.

    Holding on to relationships that bring you down is toxic. To build a great business, you must be very deliberate about who you let into it.

    Negative toxic people are everywhere, but most of the time we need not be in a relationship with them.

    Negativity is toxic to your life. A proverb states *"Walk with the wise, you become wise, associate with fools and you get in trouble"*.

    Toxic or negative people can come in multiple forms: They can be judgmental, greedy, arrogant, seeking perfection, act as victims, pessimistic to the point of where the sun never rises in their land, and have 101 excuses on why they never achieved their dreams.

    They need constant attention and suck your energy, they enjoy the attention they are getting no matter how bad it is, they gossip about everyone around, some will envy you, or some self-righteous that always feel they are right and no one else is.

The more successful you are, the more some will alienate you, envy you. When you succeed, some will become jealous of you and your success, and will either try to put you down, make fun of you or even hate you. Or some that will never let you forget past mistakes. They never let you live down who you used to be or how often you've messed up.

Stay far from these people, you need all the positive energy for your entrepreneurial journey, it is part of the journey.

Ignore them and just keep charging forward.

32. *Learning to say NO* Gurus and experts do not talk to you about it or how will come time to fire clients or refuse work.

Most of us if not all of us want to be pleasant to everyone or want to be liked by everyone or not disappoint anyone.

Whatever we are asked to do we say "YES" even if we can't or if we will waste our time, or if it will derail our own plans to succeed.

Entrepreneurs must learn to be assertive saying NO in a positive way. Not everyone will like it; especially if they are used to you accepting to do everything and anything asked of you. Some people will reject you or will let you out of their lives, know that it is fine.

The ability to say "no" will come from your ability to be clear about your goals, plans, and agenda that you want to achieve so they do not get derailed. The more you accept on your plate, the more you dilute what you are doing, you can only stretch so far.

Remember that saying "yes" to something means saying "no" to something else that might be crucial to your success.

Notice that the more successful you become, the more people will likely ask to pick your brain or ask you for free advice repeatedly to the point of eating up your time.

So be prepared the more you achieve, the more you will probably have to say "no."

It doesn't make you a bad person though some will think that you changed, or your success got to your head, or all that you care about is making money.

You can say "no" is a positive way by explaining why you must say "no"; it is an art that can be learned and practiced.

At certain times also, you will either refuse work if a client is disrespecting you or wants your services or products for a small percentage of what it is worth.

You might also need to fire clients if they are not aligned with your values or what they need challenges your non-negotiables

33. *Be of service.* Most gurus and experts talk about Entrepreneurship as getting into a business to achieve success, to leave a legacy, to support our families and to make money; which are all true and valid statements.

But, we can't get caught in only the "making money" part, we must thrive to accomplish something bigger than ourselves, we have no excuses anymore, we are not controlled by what we do, we are our own master.

First, we can't feel guilt or shame for the money we make; we paid a huge price to be where we are today.

But, we must remember to have a meaning behind our business; it must be something useful, or impactful to other people's lives.

One of the biggest mistakes some entrepreneurs do is that they focus too much on themselves versus how to help or be of service to other people.

Yes, we become entrepreneurs to make money even more money than we worked our jobs.

The difference is that being an entrepreneur is about the action of giving to others and serving them first, as a result of the value we offer we get value back from it making money.

The more you are perceived as a person or entrepreneur that helps others the more you will grow and get referrals, hence make more money.

It might sound oxymoron, but it is the safest and fastest way to achieve our dreams.

You can do it one step at a time, the journey of 1000 miles starts with one step, but that step must be taken and the journey must be started; you can't get to the finish line before passing through the starting line.

ALWAYS be of service in everything you introduce into the

market.

34. *Believe it to see it.* Most people believe that they must first see things happen, so they can believe they are happening.

It is actually the other way around, you can't see it if you don't believe it can happen, as even if it does and we believe that it will not happen, we will not see it.

We must keep our positive thinking and have a vision and believe in it so much we can actually see it, only then it will unravel in front of our very eyes.

When you believe that you can achieve whatever you set your mind to do, not only you will succeed in your business, but you will also improve the quality of your life by tapping into the power that lies within you using positive thinking to choose your destiny. This is not a "Hocus Pocus" idea, but using proven techniques, it has been established that we all can make your most impossible dreams come true.

Through belief, we can make our life anything we want it to become, including turning obstacles into opportunities; overcoming our self-limiting beliefs and develop self-confidence.

"What you focus on expands". You can achieve whatever you set your mind to do.

But you must first to set your mind for success and winning. We attract what we think about, if we believe in doom and gloom this is what we will get, and we will justify everything that happens through it, but when we have faith and believe positive outcomes this is what we will get, to see it we must believe it.

"And, when you start something, all the universe conspires in helping you to achieve it: Paulo Coelho- The Alchemist

35. *Be greedy with your time*: It sounds counter-intuitive to say be of service and be greedy with your time. Actually, they are not contradicting.

Your time becomes more and more of a commodity, you can't afford to lose a lot.

Many will try to "pick your brain" for hours ignoring this is how you make your living.

You must be conscious of that, be of service but limit the time, they can start paying you after the free counsel.

If not, you will expand yourself thin, where you will not have time for you or even for your paying customers that help you support your family.

It is not about refusing to help others, it is not about being greedy or selfish, but it is about establishing a business that is your way of living.

Limit your phone calls to fifteen minutes, try to substitute a lunch for a coffee meeting or even better for a video conference.

Set an online meeting calendar as "Calendly" for 15 or 30 minutes meetings/phone calls

36. *Delegate and outsource*: Gurus and Experts do not touch the

delegation or outsourcing concepts.

As entrepreneurs, most of us start our business on a bootstrap budget; so, we try to do everything ourselves even what we no experience in.

Our learning curves cost us a lot of money even if not noticeable at the time. We might learn and we might mess up again costing us more money.

Have a mindset that *"sometimes we need to spend money to save money"*.

Paying a professional gets the job done properly, on time and for less overall money. At the beginning of the business, use your free resources as LinkedIn and look within your connections who can barter services with you, both your businesses will help each other, and you can recommend each other at the end of the project, this way you hit two birds with one stone.

Or for a little money, you can hire a professional through sites like Freelancer, or Fiverr to do whatever you need to be done for a fraction of time and money.

Later, delegating functions of the business either through outsourcing or hiring employees increases our spectrum and reach.

Outsource everything you can, so you can **focus on doing what only you can do** in your business.

37. *Work-life balance is an illusion* and doesn't exist, especially when our professional and personal lives are becoming blended due to the

technology advancement where there is a new understanding that work is not *separate from* but *part of* life.

Gurus and Experts keep warning you of ignoring having work-life balance to avoid burn-outs.

While in theory, it is true, but in practicality, it is not. There is NO 50/50 work-life balance as entrepreneurs, somehow, we will find ourselves working or thinking about our business ALL the time.

As an entrepreneur, you must be constantly learning, processing new information, meeting deadlines, tweaking your plans, and making decisions.

If you burn yourself out, you will not have the perspective and clarity you need to guide your business in the right direction.

It is about prioritization. Set YOUR priorities. *For example,* is family your priority then no matter what; you make sure to spend the time you need with the family. It will never be 50/50 but a sense of work-life balance can be done with prioritization.

38. *Play the part, dress the part, dress your brand, and drive the part.*

It is about perceptions. People have their own perceptions about success, they attribute success to the way you dress, behave, even to the car you drive.

Though it might not be easy to maintain all that initially, but you must be mindful. Always, always dress the part. If you are going to sign a multi-thousand contract do not drive a 10-year-old beat up car. Rent a car for the day. People's Perceptions are not realities, but they are their realities. We see the world as we are, not as it is.

If you are attending an important meeting and are under-dressed the impression you will leave is that either you are lazy, disrespectful or you do not have enough money to buy clothing so maybe your business is not stable, hence not a good idea to do business with you.

Unfortunately, we live in a world where it is all about appearances, it is superficial, granted, but it is a reality.

Even if you work from home, dress your brand, you will meet people on your way to the post office or to get coffee and you can never know who you will meet, maybe your biggest customer yet.

39. *Do not start without a GREAT CPA and a better lawyer.* No matter what you do, never start your business before consulting with a good accountant or CPA.

Learn what is taxable, what is not, how you can handle the books, what is profit & loss, what is the balance sheet, and how to keep receipts, etc.

You need an even better lawyer to take you through the steps of the legalities of the business, which form you need to start your business, and the difference between the different entities as a solo proprietor, partnership, Limited Liability Company (LLC), S or C Corp and the different taxation for each. Setting your business entity up properly will have substantial implications.

Share a copy of your contracts with the lawyer, a copy of your leases, if any, etc. to make sure that not only you are covered but that you are doing the right legal moves.

CPAs and lawyers complement each other, the intertwining for legal and tax issues is complicated on its own, needing all the help you will need.

You can interview both before hiring them, check their status with the bar association and through the state licensing board.

40. *Build it and they will come is so Démodé.* It is not about just getting a DBA, or an LLC or a C or S Corporation.

It is not about having a great concept or a greater vision. It is not about getting a website with all the bells and whistles and wait for the phone to ring. Nowadays it takes a lot more than that.

Starting with SEO (Search Engine Optimization) of the website, leads generating, building lists, using the proper keywords, building credibility, building an online brand and keep refining it as you go.

Just opening an online store or a physical location thinking that the clients will come in that way, doesn't work anymore.

We live in an era full of distractions we must be in front of the customers all the time.

Many startups and small businesses either never got off the ground or failed just because they believed in building it and they will come, just because you think your product, or your services are out there doesn't guarantee that consumers will come and buy it, but without equally great promotion they are as good as non-existent.

It is simply a matter of marketing, branding, and distribution, putting your product or services in front of the eyes of the proper niche of customers. Better to have a functional website than a glitzy one.

41. Always *work on your communication skills.*

They say you can buy in any language but when you sell you must sell in the customer's language; meaning using the same words, following their culture, and terminology they use, so the marketing content on your offline and online marketing pieces should match your clients' language and culture (not necessarily a foreign language).

You need to learn to read people and be comfortable with being uncomfortable. Communication skills also include body language and non-verbal communication as smiling, looking at people in the eye without being confrontational, observing personal space, etc.

For example, when you communicate with women customers it is always better to market to them communicating through their life stages rather than their generations meaning catering to their teenage, high school student, college student, fiancé, bride to be, wife, mother, grandmother, etc.

Learn the role of values, beliefs, symbols, cultures, and even numbers in your marketing communication, communicating to Asian customers avoid using the number "4" as it is unlucky or invokes the word death.

Communicating through colors in your branding as a website, logos, and stationaries is crucial as well. For instance, you use different colors on your website, blog, and logo branding when you communicate with men customers than women customers.

42. *Networking will accelerate your growth*: Gurus and experts do not approach the subject of networking. As entrepreneurs you must grow your circle of influence, so you need to meet as many people as you can.

Networking events are great for that, just choose the right events you spend your time at. Attend events where your customers will be not just your peers.

Networking is a valuable way to develop and gain knowledge through the trails, errors, and success of others, and you can avoid yourself a lot of heartaches.

Networking can help you brand your business, meet new clients and promote your business

Talking to the right person can be a hundred times more beneficial than trying to learn on your own.

Business networking is one of the most effective technique to create pre-qualified referrals.

The advantage of networking is that it makes you visible raising your profile that can get you more leads.

You can also meet investors or influential partners.

Networking can be online or offline in real life.

43. *A partnership can be good or not:* If you decide to take partners, keep in mind that it might or might not work, too many partners can act against you especially if skills are not complementing each other.

Also, too many cooks in the kitchen, if there are many opinions the business effectiveness will become diluted and pulled in different ways.

People are different, family ties can become strained, friendships will be tested. The nightmare is if the partners or some of them do not get along.

The best way to treat a partnership is treating it like a marriage and not taking it lightly especially if you have a strong vision and used to be always in control.

Partners should complement each other like "Yin and Yang", complement each other skills, strengths, and weaknesses.

Partners should be able to trust each other, depend on each other, respect each other and go through the good, bad and ugly together.

Best way to start a partnership is to draw a contract out and sign it before the business launches.

44. *You must manage people and be a leader.* Gurus and Experts keep preaching your growth, but they never say what comes with that growth, the pain of recruiting and hiring staff.

You must also manage them, your leadership skills will be tested.

Your leadership style will dictate the failure or success of the business. Managing people is no joke and is no small task.

Entrepreneurs, by definition, are people managers. They hire staff, coach them, train them, motivate them and harness their skills and talent to benefit the business.

Managing and leading people is as much an art as it is a set of principles and tactics.

Being a leader, you as an entrepreneur must define each employee's role and job description to fit in the overall purpose of the company and not as an end in itself or a standalone function.

You also must instill in each staff member how and where they fit in the big picture of the business and establish an understanding that the end result depends upon everyone in the business working together.

As a leader, you will need to make difficult decisions that some might not like, but you are not into the "like me" business at any cost. You must have clear values and vision and be able to share them with your staff with clarity and inspire them to see the business and its mission in the same way that you do.

You will be accountable and responsible for everything that happens in the business, no room to have excuses or blame anyone else. You are at the wheel.

15. *You will get burned out*: Another point Gurus and experts do not talk about. Entrepreneurship is emotionally and physically draining.

71

You will be stressed, stretched to the max and you will still keep going either because you do not have a choice, or you made the choice to push to get to the success you dream of.

You will feel exhausted or frustrated with your business as well. The best thing you can learn is to know what drains you, what triggers your hot buttons and know how to recognize stress or fatigue when they start happening.

Educate yourself on how to distress yourself, we all have something that levels us, walking, jogging, music, driving, dancing no matter what it is, make sure once you hit a threshold to practice it to avoid burn out.

Most important is to know when to unplug, to totally unplug is going away for a weekend, with no access to cell phones, emails or even laptops.

Knowing when to take breaks during the day as in 90/10/90 working 90 minutes, breaking for 10 then repeat it again. You do not only increase your personal productivity but keeps you away from burning out.

Some people find relaxation and peace in meditation or yoga. And in breathing exercises.

46. The biggest mistake entrepreneurs do when they start, is that they *try to cast a net on everyone* thinking that appealing to everyone is the right thing to do, and the only way to make a whole lot of money.

They think that the more they try to attract to their products or services, the more diluted their message will be, and the more it will fall on deaf ears.

This couldn't be more false. When you market to everyone you market to no one. The Jake of all trades is master of none.

You will never appeal to everyone no matter what you do. Many entrepreneurs resist that notion as they feel it limits them.

You can't be the best at everything on the planet, it is just impossible.

Becoming a specialist in one area is how you can set yourself apart from the competition and what will make you unique.

When a niche is defined, your message as an entrepreneur will become clear and focused. Your niche will feel you specifically understand their problem and that it is all about them as you understand what they need and where they are coming from.

You must choose your audience, pinpoint your niche.

Customers see niche businesses as specialists, so they tend more to pay a premium price for what they perceive to be a higher level of expertise than they would get from a generic brand.

The higher prices, the higher revenues, the greater profitability. "Riches in Niches"

This makes 'going to work' a much more rewarding experience.

47. Entrepreneurs *get tunnel vision and get into their own heads*: They produce products they think are important, and makeup all the

reasons why their services are the best, or their product will disrupt the market.

They think through their own wants and needs and forget that they actually are catering to a market; to an audience that knows what they want and what they need, and sometimes it is at the other end of what the entrepreneur thinks their customers need.

Entrepreneurs fail to survey the market, I have seen many that never looked at their competition and still think they are the best on the market.

It is not about how much you believe that your business idea is viable, you must care more about the problem you are trying to solve or the gap you are trying to fill for your audience.

Also, instead of focusing on revenue or doing tasks that will increase revenue or reduce costs, entrepreneurs get busy with establishing every social media account possible or keep redesigning their website or logos.

"Always remember the rules of the road

» No one cares about you

» No one cares about your product or service

» No one cares about what you know but what your customers think, want and need

48. Gurus and experts stress the point that obviously you must make money, and *you must price your product or your service properly*, not

too high to alienate it from the market, and not too low to lose money. But they never tell you how to do it.

The biggest challenge I have seen entrepreneurs and start-ups suffer from is how to price their products or their services.

They have a hard time coming up with what is the perfect price for their products or services. They might know the competition prices, but do not know if pricing their products and services should be higher or lower than the competition.

They are under the illusion of coming up with the perfect price, and still have no clue how to propose their rates either by the hour or as a package, as a result, they lose business or money or it becomes a vicious circle.

Or they think that the only way to compete is to offer prices lower than the competition and this is the beginning of the end.

Some entrepreneurs pull the price out of thin air. Believe it or not, they do. It is also the reason many businesses fail.

Your audience will pay if they understand clearly how you can make their lives better or how you are solving their problems or how different and unique you are from your competition.

Customers pay for the "perceived value" of what you offer, that is why Corvettes, BMWs, and Rolls-Royces have a market and KIA, Hyundai, and Toyota Yaris have a market, though they are all cars that drive from one point to the other. It is all about the perceived value.

There are different ways to calculate your prices either through an intelligence market pricing report and comparing your product or service features to others, or by calculating all your expenses no matter how small and deciding on the profit margin you want to accomplish or may be combining both methods.

49. *Keep up with the market* and its offering but *never compare yourself to others* – know your uniqueness and stick to it, comparing yourself to others especially in the era of social media where everyone just shows the best or edited side of their lives online; it can get into your head and start a slippery downhill of envy, or depression, anxiety also settles in, and you can't help but feel you are not measuring up to everyone else, and feelings of "I am not good enough" can and will surface.

These doubts will put the brakes on your creativity, and innovation. When fear disguised as doubt sets in, your brain stops functioning clearly.

Comparing yourself to others will accentuate your insecurity because the picture we have in our heads of what, who, and how we are supposed to be.

The emphasis here is "supposed to be" supposed to be by whose measure, and what measure?

We must remember that we are not anyone else, that we are who we are, no one shared our story that is unique and will be the reason behind our success. We must OWN our story.

EPILOGUE
MISTAKES TO AVOID AND CORRECT

- **Management mistakes** as hiring the wrong employees or hiring a lot of employees from the get-go

- **Poor marketing planning**: Putting a lot of money in ads or total lack of marketing.

- **Hiring marketing and sales people too early** especially if as a start-up you are not sure of the direction you want to take.

- **Improper Inventory Control**: Either buying a lot of equipment or inventory or not having enough.

- Failure to develop a **strategic plan** like hiring a PR agency for two to four thousand a month from the get go.

Solution: For all of the above is working on your vision and do a proper business plan that includes a marketing plan and will map the future for you. Hire consultants or use free resources as SBA (Small Business Administration, SBDC: Small Business Development Centers, or SCORE) or look for solutions online, attend webinars and conferences, do the proper research.

- **Lack of experience**: In the industry, you want to start.

Solution: Learn and educate yourself about any market you are starting in, a common basic experience you need in any industry is customer service.

- **Hide behind the business**: The biggest mistake I see many entrepreneurs do is to hide behind their business, instead of being the face of their business. People need to trust you or see your credibility before they deal with your business, it is not the other way around.

  Solution: You need to get comfortable in uncomfortable situations, embrace self-branding, and learn to brag a bit about yourself.

- **Procrastinating:** Procrastination means the action of delaying or postponing something. Procrastination has many reasons like feeling overwhelmed, or not knowing what to do next or wanting to have perfection in everything we do.

  Solution: Stop thriving for perfection because it doesn't exist, you can thrive on excellence and doing your best. Perfection is rooted in fear.

  Time management will help you get through procrastination, managing yourself around time and not the other way around.

- **Distractions:** We are in an era where we are distracted every single minute, if not by the media by social media.

  We look for quick fixes, just to move to the next thing, the attention span is getting shorter and shorter

  Solution: Start setting smaller goals, set time for each, focus and concentrate. Take short breaks every 60 or 90 minutes to maintain your concentration

  Try short guided meditation thousands of videos exist on YouTube.

- Try to **perform and do everything yourself** either within your capability or not. This only wastes precious long hours you need building or expanding your business. Learning to do new things always come with a learning curve that can be short or long, that might or might not work, wasting not only time but money as well.

  Solution: Focus on your strength and outsource your weaknesses. Meaning do what you are good at and hire freelancers for what you need help with. Many online sites offer such help like ODesk, Fiverr, and Freelancer.

- Building a business, caring about only **what you care about**, offering services or products you think are good without catering to the needs and wants of your audience

  Solution: You must do the proper market intelligence research, analyzing your competition, survey your audience either online or in person.

- **Compare** your business to a huge fortune company and start saying something like "Coca-Cola doesn't do that:" I have news for you. You are not Coca-Cola or at least not yet, even if you were maybe what worked for them when they started will not work for you, different time, different era.

  Solution: Brand yourself based on your OWN Unique selling proposition, based on your own story, based on the specific needs of your own customers.

- **Giving up** too soon, looking for shortcuts, or taking the easy way out. I have met many entrepreneurs or startups that give up easy when glory or their breakthrough is around the corner, either their fear takes over or they take the easy way out and look for a job thinking they can finance their business, but this is the beginning of the end for the business.

Solution: It is important for an entrepreneur to be resilient, and to weather the storm, that doesn't mean keep hanging on and on when the ship is sinking. It is about believing in yourself and in your plan, about being well prepared, know when you need help and where to ask for it.

- **Negative thinking:** Being wrapped in your head, letting all the self-limiting beliefs control your way of thinking, predicting failure or not succeeding in every step of the way. Or it could be due to a lack of self-confidence, doubting your moves or ideas.

Solution: The brain thinking default is going towards the negative thinking. It takes energy and effort to positively think.

You can create new habits within few weeks, whenever your mind drifts to negative thinking you make a conscious effort to reset your brain to stop, start being grateful for everything that you have, gratitude will shift your mind to positive thinking, it is a process takes time.

- **Mission and vision** are just elements of the business plan. When I meet with entrepreneurs the first time, I always ask them about their vision and mission and most answer "they are in my business plan". Usually, they think that vision and mission are hollow statements you need to have on your business plan when you present it to a bank for a loan or for an investor.

Solution: Know this is "your" vision and "your" mission, they are part of the DNA of your business, they are part of who you are, and they are part of how you see your business and what you want to do with it.

The vision and mission statements should be flowing through your lips because you defined them based on your dreams and goals you have. Deal with them as part of your branding and "raison d'être".

- **Failing to be flexible** or to adapt, being rigid or hang up on your ideas or the way you do business can only hinder you from adjusting not only to the market needs but to your audience needs as well.

We live in a time where anything can change on a dime due to the evolvement of technology and the constant change in psych demographics.

Solution: Understand that the only constant in life is change so we need to embrace it. It is never easy to get out of the comfort zone as it is our protective shield from the unknown, but the reality is not that simple.

- **Failure to price** products or services properly. This is the biggest hurdle that stands in the way of entrepreneurs, startups, and small business owners. They have no idea or any benchmark on how to price their services or products. They try to keep up with the competition, bringing their prices lower to appeal to the customers, it doesn't work that way and could be the fastest way to close shop.

Solution: You must know every expenditure that goes into your business down to the percentage of utilities cost you use to offer services or products.

Know the value you add to your customers' lives, how you are unique and what problem you solve for them to command your prices. Customers do not buy products or services just because they are cheap, but they buy what either makes them feel better or what enhances their image. If not, Maserati, Rolls Royce or Rolex would have no customers

- Not understanding what **branding or marketing** is, in all honesty, most entrepreneurs have no clue what branding is and they get confused between marketing, branding, public relations, and sales. Many still live in a decade old marketing of printed flyers, postcards and printed brochures to leave behind, which doesn't work anymore

  Solution: Since Social Media took the marketing world by storm, everything we know about traditional marketing has been dying bit by bit, giving way to "pull marketing" replacing the "push marketing" we are used to. Entrepreneurs can either spend time learning the new rules of online and social media marketing or outsource a marketing coach or marketing consultant to help you, you can even barter for the services if cash is short.

- **Assuming build it, they will come**. In the past decades, entrepreneurs used to start a brick and mortar business, and start a website with all the bells and whistles and wait for customers to come in and buy their products. Today in the era of branding and psycho-demographics this principle doesn't work anymore.

  Solution: As a business owner, if you are local get involved in your community either volunteering in local nonprofits or being a part of the local chamber of commerce. Online, you must build credibility and share your expertise, and your uniqueness and how you help your customers to make their lives better to attract them to your business. Yes, a website is crucial to any business, but having a functional one with high SEO (Search Engine Optimization) is more important than the bells and whistles that might not attract any traffic.

- Choosing the **wrong business name**: Don't choose a name just because it means something to you or because it sounds quirky. Is it easy to spell and remember? Does it describe your business or its benefits?

Some entrepreneurs chose business names with nothing to do with their business, making it difficult for Google and customers to find them in online searches.

Solution: Choosing a name for your business is actually a science not just something you pick on a whim. A business name should shed clarity on what the business is, it is the most important place to use keywords that will help your target market understand what you offer. It must be concrete and not abstract, memorable, and catchy.

- **Growing too fast or too soon**: Some Entrepreneurs believe in fast expansion thinking this is how to dominate the market, or they add more inventory to grow faster, or even hire more staff than needed. Spending a lot of valuable cash at the start is never a good strategy.

Solution: Proper planning for any new business or its expansion is vital to the survival of the business. Short and long-term projections, as well as cash flow, are the foundation of any start-up or expansion. Having the proper strategy knowing where you start, where you want to be and how to fill the gap between, is a map to the future.

Final Thoughts

I shared the nightmare that precedes the entrepreneurship dream I wished someone shared with me before I started so I would be better prepared. It is not to try to steer anyone away from it. I am an entrepreneur, will always be one, and if I had to do it all over again I wouldn't change a thing.

Entrepreneurship is not for the faint heart, needs a lot of commitment and discipline, as you will own 200% of the responsibility of your family's fate Entrepreneurial life is not a walk in the park, it is possible to accomplish as long as we are prepared to what might and will happen

Be prepared, commit, be clear on who you are and where you want to be, welcome the challenges as opportunities, believe that you will be at the other side, most important, have faith you will SUCCEED ON YOUR OWN TERMS

www.ingramcontent.com/pod-product-compliance
Lightning Source LLC
Chambersburg PA
CBHW071225220526
45468CB00002B/734